"And you?
When will you begin that long journey into yourself?"
~Rumi

My Goals

Short Term:

"Setting goals is the first step in turning the invisible into the visible".
~Tony Robbins

Long Term:

"A goal is a dream with a deadline"
~Napoleon Hill

*"Yesterday I was clever, so I wanted to change the world.
Today I am wise, so I am changing myself"*
~Rumi

"Out of suffering have emerged the strongest souls; the most massive characters are seared with scars"
~Khalil Gibran

"No one is perfect – that's why pencils have erasers."

~Author Unknown

"Keep away from people who try to belittle your ambitions. Small people always do that, but the really great make you feel that you, too, can become great".

~Mark Twain

"When you are sorrowful look again in your heart, and you shall see that in truth you are weeping for that which has been your delight"
~Khalil Gibran

"Be yourself, everyone else is already taken".
~*Oscar Wilde*

"It does not matter how slow you go so long as you do not stop."

~Confucius

"Doubt is a pain too lonely to know that faith is his twin brother"
~Khalil Gibran

"Everything you need is already inside. Just do it"

~Bill Bowerman

"Once you choose hope, anything's possible."

~Christopher Reeve

"Trust in dreams, for in them is hidden the gate to eternity"
~Khalil Gibran

"If you can, help others; if you cannot do that,
At least do not harm them"
~Randy Rind

"Your living is determined not so much by what life brings to you as by the attitude you bring to life; not so much by what happens to you as by the way your mind looks at what happens"
~Khalil Gibran

"If you reveal your secrets to the wind, you should not blame the wind for revealing them to the trees"
~Khalil Gibran

"It's not what happens to you, but how you react to it that matters".

~Epictetus

"You cannot change the circumstances, the seasons, or the wind, but you can change yourself. That is something you have".

~Jim Rohn

*"Raise your words, not voice.
It is rain that grows flowers, not thunder"
~Rumi*

"I have learned silence from the talkative, toleration from the intolerant, and kindness from the unkind; yet, strange, I am ungrateful to those teachers"
~Khalil Gibran

"What you are is God's gift to you.
What you do with yourself is your gift to God."
~Author Unknown

"For attractive lips, speak words of kindness"

~Audrey Hepburn

*"When we turn to one another for counsel,
we reduce the number of our enemies"*
~Khalil Gibran

*"It does not matter how slowly you go
as long as you do not stop".
~Confucious*

"Our greatest weakness lies in giving up. The most certain way to succeed is always to try just one more time".
~Thomas A. Edison

*"You have to learn the rules of the game.
And then you have to play better than anyone else"*
~Albert Einstein

"If you can dream it, you can do it"
~Walt Disney

"You are never too old to set another goal or dream a new dream".
~C.S. Lewis

"By failing to prepare, you are preparing to fail".
~Benjamin Franklin

"Problems are not stop signs, they are guidelines".
~Robert H. Schuller

"What you get by achieving your goals is not as important as what you become by achieving your goals".
~Henry David Thoreau

"With the new day comes new strength and new thoughts"
~Eleanor Roosevelt

"In order to succeed, we must first believe that we can".
~Nikos Kazantzakis

"The key is to keep company only with people who uplift you, whose presence calls forth your best".
~Epictetus

*"I know where I'm going and I know the truth,
and I don't have to be what you want me to be.
I'm free to be what I want".*
~Muhammad Ali

"Failure will never overtake me if my determination to succeed is strong enough".
~Og Mandino

*"Do you want to know who you are? Don't ask. Act!
Action will delineate and define you".*
~Thomas Jefferson

"Do not wait; the time will never be 'just right'. Start where you stand, and work with whatever tools you may have at your command, and better tools will be found as you go along".
~George Herbert

"Without hard work, nothing grows but weeds".
~Gordon B. Hinckley

"You are not here merely making a living. You are here in order to enable the world to live more amply, with greater vision, with a finer spirit of hope and achievement. You are here to enrich the world, and you impoverish yourself if you forget the errand".
~Woodrow Wilson

"I prefer to be a dreamer among the humblest, with visions to be realized, than lord among those without dreams and desires"
~Khalil Gibran

"Never give up, for that is just the place and time that the tide will turn".
~Harriet Beecher Stowe

*"If you don't like something, change it.
If you can't change it, change your attitude. Don't complain".
~Maya Angelou*

"We are taught you must blame your father, your sisters, your brothers, the school, the teachers but never blame yourself. It's never your fault. But it's always your fault, because if you wanted to change, you're the one who has got to change"
~Katharine Hepburn

"If you want to succeed you should strike out on new paths, rather than travel the worn paths of accepted success"
~John D. Rockefeller

"Well done is better than well said"
~Benjamin Franklin

"Big shots are only little shots who keep shooting"
~Christopher Morley

*"Your talent is God's gift to you.
What you do with it is your gift back to God"*
~Leo Buscaglia

*"March on. Do not tarry. To go forward is to move toward
perfection. March on, and fear not the thorns,
or the sharp stones on life's path"*
~Khalil Gibran

"What you seek is seeking you"
~Rumi

"Learn from the past, set vivid, detailed goals for the future, and live in the only moment of time over which you have any control: Now"
~Denis Waitley

"You can never quit. Winners never quit, and quitters never win"
~Ted Turner

"The wound is the place where the Light enters you."
~Rumi

*"Stop acting so small.
You are the universe in ecstatic motion"
~Rumi*

"Never, never, never give up"
~Winston Churchill

*"Don't grieve.
Anything you lose comes around in another form"
~Rumi*

"I learned that we can do anything, but we can't do everything…at least not at the same time. So think of your priorities not in terms of what activities you do, but when you do them. Timing is everything"
~Dan Millman

"If you are irritated by every rub, how will your mirror be polished?"
~Rumi

*"I don't believe you have to be better than everybody else.
I believe you have to be better than you ever thought you could be"*
~Ken Venturi

"You were born with wings, why prefer to crawl through life?"
~Rumi

"If you don't design your own life plan, chances are you'll fall into someone else's plan. And guess what they have planned for you? Not much".
~Jim Rohn

"This being human is a guest house. Every morning is a new arrival. A joy, a depression, a meanness, some momentary awareness comes as an unexpected visitor. Welcome and entertain them all. Treat each guest honorably. The dark thought, the shame, the malice, meet them at the door laughing, and invite them in. Be grateful for whoever comes, because each has been sent as a guide from beyond"
~Rumi

*"Knowing is not enough; we must apply.
Willing is not enough; we must do".
~Johann Wolfgang von Goethe*

"Where there is a will, there is a way. If there is a chance in a million that you can do something, anything, to keep what you want from ending, DO IT. Pry the door open or, if need be, wedge your foot in that door and keep it open"
~Pauline Kael

*"When you do things from your soul,
you feel a river moving in you, a joy"*
~Rumi

"The wound is the place where the light enters you"
~Rumi

"Motivation will almost always beat mere talent"
~Norman Ralph Augustine

*"There is a candle in your heart, ready to be kindled.
There is a void in your soul, ready to be filled.
You feel it, don't you?"*
~Rumi

"Do not wait to strike till the iron is hot; but make it hot by striking".
~William Butler Yeats

"Aim for the moon. If you miss, you may hit a star"
~W. Clement Stone

*"Be empty of worrying.
Think of who created thought!*

*Why do you stay in prison
When the door is so wide open?"
~Rumi*

"Set your life on fire. Seek those who fan your flames"
~Rumi

"Whatever you want in life, other people are going to want it too. Believe in yourself enough to accept the idea that you have an equal right to it"
~Diane Sawyer

*"Live with intention. Walk to the edge. Listen hard. Practice wellness. Play with abandon. Laugh. Choose with no regret. Appreciate your friends. Continue to learn. Do what you love.
Live as if this is all there is".
~Mary Anne Radmacher*

"To be able to look back upon ones life in satisfaction is to live twice"
~Khalil Gibran

"The minute I heard my first love story, I started looking for you, not knowing how blind that was. Lovers don't finally meet somewhere. They're in each other all along"
~Rumi

"Only surround yourself with people who will lift you higher".
~*Oprah Winfrey*

"Goodbyes are only for those who love with their eyes. Because for those who love with heart and soul, there is no such thing as separation"
~Rumi

"You give but little when you give of your possessions. It is when you give of yourself that you truly give"
~Khalil Gibran

"Wisdom ceases to be wisdom when it becomes too proud to weep, too grave to laugh, and too selfish to seek other than itself"
~Khalil Gibran

"Resolve never to quit, never to give up,

No matter what the situation".

~Jack Nicklaus

"Knowledge of the self is the mother of all knowledge. So it is incumbent on me to know myself, to know it completely, to know its minutia, its characteristics, its subtleties, and its very atoms"
~*Khalil Gibran*

"Promise me you will always remember – You are braver than you believe, stronger than you seem and smarter than you think"

~Christopher Robin to Pooh

*"Sometimes in order to help He makes us cry.
Happy the eye that sheds tears for His sake.
Fortunate the heart that burns for his sake.
Laughter always follows tears.
Blessed are those who understand.
Life blossoms wherever water flows.
Where tears are shed, divine mercy is shown"
~Rumi*

"Love and doubt have never been on speaking terms"
~Khalil Gibran

"The key to everything is patience. You get the chicken by hatching the egg, not by smashing it".

~Arnold H. Glasow

"No man can reveal to you nothing but that which already lies half asleep in the dawning of your knowledge"
~Khalil Gibran

"Most people who ask for advice from others have already resolved to act as it pleases them"
~Khalil Gibran

"Reach high, for stars lie hidden in your soul.
Dream deep, for every dream precedes the goal."
~Ralph Vaull Starr

"If the grandfather of the grandfather of Jesus had known what was hidden within him, he would have stood humble and awe struck before his soul"
~Khalil Gibran

"Do what you can, with what you have, where you are."

~Theodore Roosevelt

"Sorrow prepares you for joy. It violently sweeps everything out of your house so that new joy can find space to enter. It shakes the yellow leaves from the bough of your heart so that fresh, green leaves can grow in their place. It pulls up the rotten roots so that new roots hidden beneath have room to grow. Whatever sorrow shakes from your heart, far better things will take their place"
~Rumi

"If the other person injures you, you may forget the injury; but if you injure him you will always remember"
~Khalil Gibran

"Talent is God-given. Be humble.
Fame is man-given. Be grateful.
Conceit is self-given. Be careful."
~John Wooden

*"Advance and never halt, for advancing is perfection.
Advance and do not fear the thorns in the path,
for they draw only corrupt blood"*
~Khalil Gibran

"You pray in your distress and in your need; would that you might also pray in the fullness of your joy and in your days of abundance"
~Khalil Gibran

"I am bigger than anything that can happen to me. All these things, sorrow, misfortune, and suffering, are outside my door. I am in the house and I have the key."

~Charles Fletcher Lummis

*"When you go through a hard period,
When everything seems to oppose you,
When you feel you cannot even bear one more minute,
NEVER GIVE UP!
Because it is the time and place
That the course will divert"*
~Rumi